A BOOT UP

EXMOOR

Adrian Tierney-Jones

First published in Great Britain in 2008
Copyright © 2008 Adrian Tierney-Jones

Front cover: *Heather above Shillett Wood on Porlock Common.*
© Neville Stannik from *Perfect Exmoor*

British Library Cataloguing-in-Publication Data
A CIP record for this title is available from the British Library

ISBN 978 1 906887 04 9

PiXZ Books
Halsgrove House, Ryelands Industrial Estate,
Bagley Road, Wellington, Somerset TA21 9PZ
Tel: 01823 653777
Fax: 01823 216796
email: sales@halsgrove.com

An imprint of Halstar Ltd, part of the Halsgrove group of companies
Information on all Halsgrove ttles is available at: www.halsgrove.com

Printed and bound by D'Auria Industrie Grafiche, Italy

Brian Pearce

Contents

How to use this book

The Area

Exmoor is the last great wilderness of southern England. This is a land of small isolated hamlets and villages, deep woody combes echoing to the metallic clack of the cock pheasant and the drill and tap of the wood-pecker, mysterious swathes of wood-land where the deer walk and high exposed stretches of moor that bear the full force of winter wind and rain, home to herds of shaggy-haired, obstinate Exmoor ponies.

Fast-flowing crystal clear rivers cut through the land, above which the occasional azure flash of a kingfisher can be seen – while down in the cool river-deep depths trout, grayling and the occasional salmon browse. The Bristol Channel washes the northern edge of Exmoor, with breath-taking views available in the area of Lynton and Countisbury.

This is God's own walking country, a land of contrasts, extremes even – empty and desolate in great swathes, but it remains a working land rather than a rural playground. To walk it is to be humbled by nature, nurtured and nourished by its terrible beauty. These 10 walks are but a small selection, but it is hoped that they will inspire and stimulate a deep love of Exmoor and all its workings.

The Routes

All these walks finish where they started, so you don't have to rely on scant public transport or friends or family to meet you with the car at the end; they normally start at car parks, though where possible I have put in public transport details. The lengths vary from five to eight miles and they are ideal for walks with friends and family, though some are more challenging than others; a few are all-terrain buggy friendly (providing you are happy with a couple of members of the party lugging it up rougher ground) and there are shorter versions of walks pointed out where possible; taking very young ones out on other walks might depend on how strong the backpack carrier feels.

They are graded between one and three boots, with three boots the hardest. Most involve some ascending, but we're not talking a day out on the Glyders in Snowdonia or a climb up Great Gable in the Lake District. These are walks that can be leisurely done in the morning to work up an appetite for lunch, or used as a convenient excuse to work off that lunch... Some will pass pubs or cafés, but most refreshment stops are at the start of the walk.

'Set off' also has map references and postcodes, while direction details are added in parenthesis, specifying compass points: N (north), NNE (north-northeast), NE (northeast), ENE (east-northeast), E (east), ESE (east-southeast), SE (southeast), SSE (south-southeast), S (south), SSW (south-southwest), SW (southwest), WSW (west-southwest), W (west), WNW (west-northwest), NW (northwest). Always carry a compass.

All the walks are across footpaths and other routes with public access, as existing when the book went to press: these can change; always make sure you have an up to date map. Given that Exmoor has a real sense of wildness, always make sure you have the right weather equipment.

Always take care, especially when walking along narrow seaward paths or descending rock-strewn hollow ways. Road-walking is another occasion in which to keep your wits about you. Always remember that Exmoor is a working environment and keep dogs on lead if there are stock in view; close all gates and if your path takes you past a farmhouse say hello to its occupants, you'll be surprised how friendly people can be.

The Maps

Even though a map of the route is provided it is advisable to have an Ordnance Survey map, which is essential if you get lost or want to take a short cut back. One Ordnance Survey map currently covers Exmoor and its National Park: this is Explorer OL9 (Exmoor) — it is available in most local newsagents, National Park shops and booksellers such as WH Smith's.

Key to Symbols Used

Level of difficulty:

Easy 🐑

Fair 🐑 🐑

More challenging 🐑 🐑 🐑

Map symbols:

🚗 Park & start

▬▬▬ Tarred Road

- - - - Unpaved road

----- Footpath

■ Building

+ Church

▲ Triangulation pillar or other landmark

🚻 WC

🍴 Refreshments

🍺 Pub

WALK LOCATIONS

5 Countisbury
Brendon 8
Porlock Weir
Minehead
Parracombe
Blue Anchor
Watchet
Challacombe
River Exe
7
2
Wheddon Cross
Withycombe
4
Exford
Withypool
9
6
3
Twitchen
Hawkridge
1
10
South Molton

N
W E
S

1 Haddon Wood

A delightful 5-mile ramble that takes in both woodland and part of the River Haddeo.

This is a tranquil woodland walk, ideal for families in dry weather. With strong arms you can do it with an all-terrain buggy, though the last section might be a bit tough on baby.

It will certainly wake a young one up. As well as travelling through woodland, the stroll passes through the tiny but picturesque hamlet of Hartford and takes a pleasing walk alongside the River Haddeo; there's also the chance of a detour to the pretty hamlet of Bury.

Level: 🐾
Length: 5 miles
Terrain: Woodland walk with wide well-marked trails, plus a slightly steep ascent — ideal for a family stroll on a summer's afternoon. Some rocky surfaces mean that if you take a buggy it might have to be carried.
Park & start: Park on verge by side of road opposite farm at Louisa Gate, which can be found on the road signposted Watchet at Machine Cross on the A396.
Start ref: SS904419.
Public transport: None.
Refreshments: Pubs and cafés in nearby Dulverton.

Please note: as this is predominantly conifer woodland, forestry work is carried out at certain times of the year.

[Map showing route through Storage Wood, Haddon Wood, Barlynch Wood, with waypoints 1–13, River Haddeo, River Exe, Hartford, Wimbleball Lake, and Bury]

① Park on the verge at Louisa Gate; follow the sign for Hartford, where it says permitted path. Walk down a sunken path: note, it can be muddy in the winter. After 120 metres go through a gate and follow a forest track through woodland (NE). To our right, a vast

Louisa Gate

Looking towards Hartford Bottom.

In the midst of a conifer plantation.

green swathe of trees rises up from Hartford Bottom through which the River Haddeo flows. The track descends and curves to the right. After 190 metres the road curves to the left. This is easy walking and after 440 metres the track straightens out. This is a delightful walk through mixed woodland; in the winter the coppery leaves left on the beech trees add a smattering of colour.

 After a few metres the road curves to the left, and 220 metres later pass over a stream trickling down from the direction of Lyncombe Farm. We soon meet a sign on the right — ignore and go in the direction of Hartford (NE). On a windy day, enjoy the music of the wind through the trees. The path rises. We are midst of a conifer plantation: the trees stand in ranks, spilling down the slope while crows, rooks and the odd raven sound off in high dudgeon; the leathery flap of wings denotes a startled pigeon.

3 After 430 metres we are still heading NE. The land opens out a bit and the view is across the valley towards the alpine-like mysteries of Haddon Wood with Haddon Hill rising above it. Storridge Wood is below us on the right after 360 metres: woodland of mixed species, including ash, oak, birch and ubiquitous conifers.

4 After 650 metres take the right fork of the path as it descends through Hartford Wood — this is a curvaceous path. Eighty metres on take the second track on the right, which curves and bends as it descends. After 200 metres curve to the left; a few metres later turn to the right and descend down an old hollow way, with open fields on both sides. This brings us to the hamlet of Hartford, a pretty settlement to the west of Wimbleball Lake.

5 Look for the sign in the direction of Bury, passing Hartford Lodge on our right. The track ahead is called Lady Harriet's Drive. This is straightforward walking, alongside the River Haddeo, with the Hartford Trout Farm being passed after 240 metres.

6 This is a delightful walk along Hartford Bottom, where trout can be often glimpsed snapping away at flies from the security of the river. Birdlife to be seen and heard include raucous jays, solitary herons, buzzards mewling in the sky and the occasional sparrow hawk zigzagging in and out of the trees chasing its prey.

River Haddeo.

7 Continue on this path for nearly two kilometres (SW), enjoying the wooded landscape. During dry weather this track is suitable for an off-road buggy, though there might be areas in which it would have to be carried.

8 After another 140 metres the track forks to the right, but continue left, keeping company with the river, while passing over a stream.

9 A small cottage comes into view on the left 300 metres on. Carry on straight along the path, passing another cottage shortly. After 450 metres the valley opens out with green river meadows lying below to the left.

10 After 470 metres we pass a building, which looks like a lodge. If the track is followed to the left we will arrive in Bury. However, our goal is Louisa Gate, which is signposted for the second right turning onto a rock-surfaced hollow way.

11 This is the steepest part of the climb and those with very young children might want to jump ship at Bury. After 270 metres, the way opens out and there are views of Haddon Hill to the right — on our left the old hill-fort of Bury also comes into view.

12 After 400 metres we go through a gate and the track levels out, with the ascent being somewhat gentler.

13 The return to Louisa Gate is just over a kilometre's walking over a rough, slightly stony track. This is a walk lined with grown-out and copper-coloured beech hedges, while clumps of rhododendrons are also visible. Return to Louisa Gate.

Lady Harriet's Drive was built in the late eighteenth century in honour of Lady Harriet Acland, who had rescued her husband Colonel Acland when captured by the French in the American War of Independence.

Old lodge above Bury.

Brian Pearce

Bury Bridge.

2 Nutcombe Bottom

A long but easily followed 7-mile circuit through woodland that also visits a prehistoric hill-fort.

Level: 🥾
Length: 7 miles
Terrain: Woodland walk with wide well-marked trails, a couple of slightly steep descents and one climb.

Park & start: Car park on the left hand of the road that rises from a signed turning-off on the A396, approximately a mile out of Dunster (W).
Start ref: SS976423. Postcode TA24 6TA.
Public transport: None.
Refreshments: Pubs and cafés in nearby Dunster.

A 7-mile woodland walk that offers long stretches of contemplative walking. The woodland around this walk is predominantly conifer such as larch, Scots pine, spruce and fir, initially planted in the years after World War I. Deciduous trees are represented by beech, oak and silver birch. Now owned by the Crown Estates but criss-crossed with woodland walks and trails, it is a popular environment for walkers and families, drawn by the gentle elevation, broadness of the drives/trails (used by forestry vehicles during logging) and the contemplativeness that walking through these silent woods can bring. This walk also includes a diversion to the Iron Age settlements of Bat's Castle and Gallox Hill. There are plenty of well-signed woodland paths for those who want to make the walk shorter.

Dunster Park

Whits Wood

11

12

Hats Wood

Hur Wood

10

2

1

9

8

3

7

6

4

5

Croydon Hill

① Emerge from the Nutcombe Bottom car park, turn left and ascend. Follow the road for 220 metres and turn right onto a path/bridleway. At the gate bear left and at 250 metres two paths are reached;

Nutcombe Bottom.

Towns Wood: keep an eye out for woodpeckers!

take the right one in the direction of Timberscombe. The woodland to the left is Towns Wood and is home to various birdlife including the great spotted woodpecker.

 ② The path gently ascends after 430 metres and a forest track

is reached. Turn right — tall conifers line the path in untidy ranks, this is a landscape fashioned by man. After 540 metres arrive at a junction, turn right and bear to left; follow path round, through thinned out woodland. On your right there is a wire fence with a field beyond and views to the northwest including Wootton Courtney village; 520 metres on, we are in open country, keep following the path ahead.

3 Turn left after another 320 metres, ascend gently along this trail (SE), back into the midst of conifers, note the deer trails disappearing into the thick clumps of trees. The main road on which we parked further down appears 330 metres on; cross and go through gate opposite (SE). Keep bearing right; on a sunny day sunbeams penetrating into the crowd of trees have the appearance of thin smoke. Continue walking ahead, this is a mystery-laden, contemplative walk as the dense rows of conifers march down to the track.

4 After 940 metres, the path opens up to the light: the trees here are younger. For a detour there is a path on the right up to Croydon Hill. Otherwise, keep on the main path, before arriving at a signpost after 870 metres. Follow the direction to Perley Combe (SE). After 670 metres we come to a cross-paths with a gate on the left.

Continue towards Perley Combe.

Open moorland rises ahead. Turn left through the gate and left again following the path alongside the fence line on the left. This is a descent on the western side of Black Hill, a traditional Exmoor moorland landscape of bracken, gorse and scattered clumps of hawthorn sculptured into tortured images by the wind.

5 After 540 metres, pass the clearance of Withycombe Scruffets, where woodland once supplied charcoal and tan bark. The path continues to descend and after 800 metres we come to a gate on the left. Go through the gate, noting the information board about Black Hill and straight ahead there is a path into woodland (N-NE).

Descend down this well-trodden path passing through mainly broadleaf trees, noting the blueway marks. After 490 metres, we come to another path on the left, with a field to the right; a few metres to the left a path turns to the left to go through woodland. This is a steepish descent through a

Bat's Castle is a prehistoric hill-fort that is thought to have been built between 400-100BC; in 1983 a small hoard of coins dating from 102BC-350AD was discovered in the ramparts there.

standing army of tall pines and broadleaf trees. Be careful if balance is a problem.

At 470 metres, we come to a meeting of five paths, alongside Long Combe stream. Take the second path on right, signed Dunster; the stream and field are on our left as we ascend.

Nutcombe Plantation.

Nutcombe Plantation.

8 After 490 metres, during which we have crossed a stream feeding into Long Combe, we briefly veer left signed Dunster and Nutcombe before seeing ahead of us a track rising through woodland (N). This will eventually take us to Bat's Castle, an Iron Age encampment.

Brian Pearce

Bat's Castle.

9 Follow the path up with red and blue arrows pointing the way; keep climbing, noting the old Exmoor stone walls with trees growing out. At 220 metres we get to a gate on the right, ascending through a thick wood of conifers that crowd the path. Follow the path up and after 320 metres we get to open common-land, follow the path curving to the left, keeping the woodland to the left; after 410 metres turn left and a few metres on there is Bat's Castle. Tremendous views over Dunster and the coast towards Wales are the reward.

10 Follow the path through Bat's Castle (NW). After 640 metres we dip into a small but wide combe, where an old 'Horse Road' path comes up from the right — it

Brian Pearce

Gallox Hill.

would have come up from Dunster. Continue forward to Gallox Hill, passing another settlement. It's a gentle climb and the path curves round the right side of the settlement, which is now overgrown though its ditches are visible.

11 Take time to admire the Wagnerian splendour of Grabbist Hill ahead (NW); after 490 metres we follow the path as it descends into woodland. We now descend down through mixed woodland, with an old Exmoor stone wall on the left. After 120 metres bear left on the trail with the wall still on our left; passing a wooden sculpture to the left – is it a bear or a pig?

12 After 230 metres we come to a cross-path; take the first right, descending through more conifers. After 380 metres we reach a road, which goes up to Broadwood Farm, hence the name Broadwood Road, take its left branch, pass over a stream; after 170 metres take the track on the right and 320 metres will see us back at the car park.

Wooden sculpture: a bear or a pig?

3 **Tarr Steps**

This is a challenging 8½-mile trek over moorland, through woodland and alongside Dane's Brook.

This is a stimulating and challenging trek that starts at one of Exmoor's most historic and popular spots before going up and down hill and across moorland, as well as being interspersed with a

According to local legend the Tarr Steps were built by the Devil to win a bet.

spot of riverside rambling. The reward is beautiful scenery and immense views towards the south-west from Anstey Gate. This is truly an Exmoor classic.

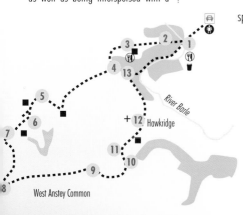

Level: 🐾 🐾 🐾
Length: 8½ miles
Terrain: A bracing mixture of moorland, woodland and riverside walking, necessitating some road work but the rewards include crossing the historic Tarr Steps, close contact with Exmoor ponies on Anstey Common, stupendous views southwards towards Dartmoor at Anstey Gate and the upland village of Hawkridge – this is one of the longest walks in the book so make sure you are well-equipped, though it's not as challenging as a trek on the Chains.
Park & start: Park at Tarr Steps car park and follow the signs towards the Steps.
Start ref: SS873324.
Postcode: TA22 9PY.
Public transport: None.
Refreshments: Tarr Steps Farm.

① Set-off from Tarr Steps car park follow directions to the Steps, passing Tarr Farm on the right. After 460 metres we come to the Tarr Steps over the Barle. Once across follow the sign pointing right towards Withypool and Hawkridge. After 190 metres we follow the path on the right, with a house down below us to the left. The path climbs and after 320 metres we pass through a gate and wheel to the right.

② We pass through another gate at 200 metres (N), turn left into a field and walk up (W) with the hedge on our left. We go through a gate on our left after 360 metres and

The path to Parsonage Farm.

Some think Tarr Steps to be of prehistoric origin but they are more likely to have been built in the Middle Ages according to the latest theories. Hawkridge is home to the 'Antler Man' Tom Lock, who carves items from deer antlers.

Tarr Steps.

turn immediately right through a gate following the sign 'Parsonage Farm Refreshments'. Keep going through the field with the hedge to your left (W). The walk levels out. Note: there might be stock in the field so keep any dogs on a lead. There is another gate at 410 metres, go through it and we start ascending.

3 We pass a sign in the direction of Hawkridge at 190 metres, and go through Parsonage Farm's yard with barns to the right and the farm itself down on the left. Keep on following directions for Hawkridge. The track curves to the left after 450 metres, we cross a small brook and start rising through woodland. After 330 metres we reach a tarmac road and turn right.

Tarr Post.

Alternatively you can turn left and follow the signs back to Tarr Steps if you want to make this a brief walk.

4 We continue on this road for over a kilometre (SE), passing Huntercombe Farm on the right before arriving at Tarr Post. Here we turn left, walk a few more metres on the road, and turn right into a field following the signs for Anstey

Gate. There are glorious views over Anstey Common. After 270 metres the path curves to the left (S), while after 160 metres we turn right into a large field and walk ahead with the fence on our left.

5 After 190 metres go through the gate on the left, turn right and follow the fence to your right. We curve round to the left at 300 metres and follow the direction pointing to

Cloggs Farm.

Bridge at Dane's Brook.

Lyshwell (S-SW). Cloggs Farm is on our right as we descend through a small partially wooded valley. Keep following the direction signposted Anstey Gate and at 480 metres we get to a wooden footbridge over the bright and bubbly stream called Dane's Brook.

(6) Cross the bridge and start climbing. Make for a line of trees on your right, about 400 metres away. Go through the gate, turn right and pass Lyshwell Farm on your right. Note the sound of the generator: the farm is one of the few on Exmoor still not connected to the mains. Follow a path past the generator shed on our left and then the farm. It curves right and then straightens out a few metres to the left.

(7) After 140 metres the track curves to the left over a stream and then starts ascending. After 300 metres it levels out and behind us there are impressive views towards Winsford Hill and the moorland over which you have just walked. A steady walk of 620 metres eventually takes us to Anstey Gate with immense views over northern Devon, especially towards Dartmoor.

Looking over West Anstey Common in the direction of Hawkridge.

West Anstey Common.

Brian Pearce

(8) Turn left then take the path over the moorland travelling in a NE direction. It descends; listen out for larks in the spring and summer. The path is occasionally boggy. Keep on the path and at 650 metes we pass through a gap in a small line of gorse. You should see Exmoor ponies on the common. After 590 metres we are starting to see clumps of gorse, hardy moor trees and hear the sound of running water from Dane's Brook below.

(9) The brook is reached after 430 metres. There is a ford that is deep in winter and not recommended, so turn right and follow the footpath alongside the river, passing through gatherings of birch, oak and holly, plus the odd fallen tree.

(10) The going can be slightly boggy in parts, but after a kilometre we reach Slade Bridge. This is a delightful old single-arched stone bridge: the boundary between Devon and Somerset goes through the centre. Turn left onto the road and follow it upwards, passing the entrance to Zeal Farm on the left.

Slade Bridge.

Tarr Steps

In 1952 all but one span of Tarr Steps was swept away during the same heavy rain that devastated Lynmouth on the other side of Exmoor.

 After 490 metres we go through the gate on the right, which is sign-posted Hawkridge. Take a NE direction across the field, heading for several large trees and a building. After 300 metres pass through a gate onto a road and head right and then bear left into the village of Hawkridge. On getting to the centre turn left at the junction, noting the old tree in the centre of the road and the seat built into it. Follow the directions to Withypool and after 120 metres turn right in the direction of Tarr Steps, through a gate, down a path and over a stile.

 Follow the yellow markers across two fields (N) for 400

Hawkridge.

Brian Pearce

metres until you come to woodland on our right called Great Cleeve. After 200 metres we take a stile over the fence, taking the path that levels out to the right: it can be muddy in the winter.

We descend gently through three fields, keeping the woodland to our right (Parsonage Farm can be glimpsed across the way); after 590 metres we reach a gate and a sign for Penny Bridge. Turn right and descend along the rocky surface through evergreen woodland. After 380 metres we come to a road, turn left for Tarr Steps. This is easy road walking with the Barle on the right; after 900 metres we get to Tarr Steps. Follow the signs back to the car park.

4 **Cow Castle**

An occasionally demanding 8¾-mile walk that starts alongside the Barle before climbing onto classic Exmoor moorland scenery.

This is a pulsating perambulation through some of Exmoor's finest moorland scenery. As a bonus, the route also passes the venerable and

A local legend once credited the building of Cow Castle to moorland pixies.

ancient Iron Age hill-fort of Cow Castle as well as the ruins of Wheal Eliza, the site of a gruesome discovery in 1858 of a little girl's brutally murdered body — her father was eventually executed for this horrible crime.

Level: 🌾 🌾
Length: 8¾ miles
Terrain: An enchanting trek that starts in Simonsbath, forever associated with the Knight family, who did so much to transform the Exmoor Forest in the nineteenth century. The first part follows the Barle in a steep-sided, bracken-covered valley. The walk begins its climb above the river onto grassy moorland, before taking the path back towards Simonsbath over Winstitchen Hill.
Park & start: there is a signed car park near the Exmoor Forest Hotel, or park on the verge at the start of the walkl.
Start ref: SS774393.
Postcode: TA24 7SH.
Public transport: None.
Websites: www.whatsonexmoor.co.uk/villages/simonsbath.htm
Refreshments: Exmoor Forest Hotel. Boevey's

Simonsbath

Winstitchen Farm

Two Moors Way

River Barle

25

① Walk to Birch Cleave Wood and follow the path through woodland; the Barle will be on our right. Continue on this track, passing through a gate at 360 metres. At 610 metres pass through another gate and walk over a stream emptying into the Barle. This is a scoured landscape – bleak in the winter, with water everywhere and exposed stone looking like old castle walls; a giant garden designer gone mad.

Birch Cleave Wood.

The Barle at Flexbarrow.

② The path starts a gentle ascent at 480 metres and the river momentarily vanishes and loops round Flexbarrow; we keep to the left with the barrow (which is natural rather than manmade) on our right. After 270 metres we pass the ruins of Wheal Eliza on our left; deer are often seen on the slopes above. Pass through a gate in a few metres. Pass through another gate in 370 metres and after 720 metres the path is right next to the Barle, with the rock formation almost a pavement.

3   After passing through a stretch that is almost Alpine

with its trees and steep rock, we come to a mature, grown-out hedge-line of trees in 200 metres. Follow either the blueway sign or the line of trees, keeping the river on our right. The landscape

Wheal Eliza ruins.

Brian Pearce

The Wheal Eliza copper and iron ore mine ran from 1846 to 1855 and was not a success; its shaft was also the site where William Burgess dumped the body of his murdered daughter in 1858.

Brian Pearce

The Barle below Wheal Eliza.

Brian Pearce

Cow Castle.

opens out in 480 metres and Cow Castle lies ahead (SE).

(4) The Barle curves away to the right to loop around Cow Castle after 520 metres. We take the path to the left. Cow Castle is worth a detour or this could be the ideal place for those of us with youngsters to turn back, but not before a swim in the river in the summer. Follow the well-trodden path with Cow Castle to the right. Across the valley to our left, the Pickedstones Plantation climbs up the slope.

(5) After 170 metres the path gentle ascends, taking a route (S-SE) between Cow Castle on our right and the small hillock opposite; this is often called the Calf. This path is easy to follow using the blueway posts. Make for a gate, which we reach after 400 metres. Cross the stile and bridge over White Water, which

Birch Cleave Wood is the highest beech wood in England and was planted by the Knights in the 1850s.

Bridge over the Barle.

feeds into the Barle, and make for the bridge that crosses the Barle; we will not be crossing it though.

(6) Here follow the directions to Withypool, keeping the Barle on your right and the plantation on your left. After 180 metres blueway markings direct us through the plantation on an easily identified path (NE).

Follow in the direction of Simonsbath.

7 After 550 metres we get to a gate and out of the wood. Follow a path signed Withypool and Pickedstones. The path starts a gentle ascent through a landscape of open moorland surrounded by undulating hills. We say goodbye to the Barle. The clearly marked track starts to climb after 440 metres, curving to the right (NE) in 730 metres.

8 At 730 metres turn left, following the direction to Simonsbath and Pickedstones. For the next 1100 metres travel west along the top edge of the valley enjoying the views, before coming to a gate.

Keep on following directions to Simonsbath and Pickedstones, heading across the field, aiming for the gate in the lower left corner. Here turn left onto a concreted track. A few metres ahead we pass through

The view towards Winstitchen.

Brian Pearce

a gate, Pickedstones farm to our right, barn to left.

9 We get to a gate and enter a path that passes below the farm's garden; walk along the path and there is another gate straight ahead. Turn right here, following the path with the hedge line on our right. After 320 metres we go through a gate and follow a path which curves round a small shallow combe with a spring. The path bears left and descends; this is straightforward easy walking. After 570 metres the path goes over White Water, curves to the right, then turns left and starts to climb.

 10 A blueway-marked path appears on the left at 460 metres. Turn left and head towards a

line of trees (W). After 80 metres follow the signpost to Simonsbath, passing conifer woodland to the right. Pass through a gap in the old hedge line and continue ahead. We are on top of Winstitchen Hill and when the wind blows it is ferocious.

11 We come to a gate after 460 metres, go through and keep following the path with the hedge on right. After 570 metres we are still following the signs to Simonsbath, passing Winstitchen Farm on the right. Walk in a NE direction towards an old shed. After 40 metres go through a gate into a field following the hedge line on the right.

12 Keep following the path and signs towards Simonsbath

Beeches in Birch Cleave Wood.

and after 850 metres we turn left onto a path signed Simonsbath; we are in Birch Cleave Wood and the walk becomes a gentle descent. Note the woodcarvings. After 90 metres the path veers right and 350 metres on we are back where we started.

5 **Lynton**

A pleasing 5½-circuit starting off in the town of Lynton with plenty of inspiring sea views

A gentle and tranquil walk that starts off in Lynton. The walk is a blend of seaward views and rocky mountain highs as it turns inwards from its wind-swept path above the Bristol Channel into the Valley of Rocks before rising and returning into the town by Lydiate Lane, which was formerly the road to Barnstaple. This is an ideal family walk, though it is highly recommended that a careful eye be kept on toddlers on the path out of Lynton and dogs remain on leads – wild goats run free in the Valley of Rocks. For a shorter trek turn left at the Valley of Rocks and follow the signs back to Lynton. It is level until the Valley of Rocks, then climb steadily until Six Acres Cross sees it return down Lydiate Lane.

Level: 🐾

Length: 5½ miles

Terrain: A pleasant and undemanding walk with grand sea views and the strange rock shapes of the Valley of Rocks, with a sharp but not too challenging climb through woodland and open moorland. Very easy to follow and the reward is the sound and sight of the sea and the weird assemblage of rock shapes.

Park & start: Park in Lynton's lower car park at Bottom Meadow.

Start ref: SS722494.

Postcode: EX35 6JA.

Public transport: Barnstaple-Lynton, 309, 310.

Websites: www.lynton-lynmouth-tourism.co.uk; www.lyntonandlynmouth.org.uk

Refreshments: Plenty of pubs and cafés in Lynton & Lynmouth.

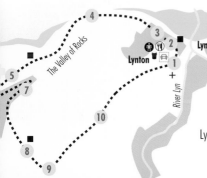

1 We make our way out of the car park, turn left up Church Hill and walk towards the parish church of St Mary. Turn right after 220 metres, down North Walk Hill between St Mary and the Valley Rocks Hotel, following the sign for the Valley of Rocks. To our right there are views of the magnificent Lynmouth Bay — high cliffs rising towards Countisbury. Down below, we get a glimpse of Lynmouth and the grey-blue thread of the Lyn passing into the sea.

2 The path levels out at 160 metres and we pass over the track of the funicular that dives giddily down towards Lynmouth. Sea-facing hotels are passed, such as the

Lynmouth Bay.

Brian Pearce

Funicular railway that links Lynton and Lynmouth.

Castle Rock.

Chough's Nest Hotel, evidence of Lynton's long reliance on tourism. On a windy day, down far below, the sound of the sea is reminiscent of heavy rain drumming its fingers impatiently on tin roofs. Continue on the same path and at 460 metres we

pass through an entrance; a sign reminds walkers that dogs should be kept under control as goats are grazing. The land slopes down steep to the sea on the right.

 There is another gate at 160 metres as we pass through beech woodland. The trees are soon left behind and bare rocky moorland rises to the left while the land drops away steeply to the right. Hollerday Hill rises further to the left. After 620 metres we reach a signpost pointing in the direction of Castle Rock. Follow this. The landscape is dominated by untidy groups of craggy rock. Descend past the remains of an old rusty gate.

4 The path descends slightly and at 500 metres we get our

The funicular railway that drops from Lynton to Lynmouth is one of the few water-powered railways in the world; it was opened in 1888.

first sighting of Wringcliff Bay with the immense towering mass of Castle Rock on the left. The open expanse of the Valley of Rocks is reached at 220 metres: this is a landscape of heather, gorse, bare moorland, gigantic rock formations and wild goats; note the path up to Castle Rock, it is not recommended on a windy day. We get to a road roundabout, take the right branch (SW).

Goats in the Valley of Rocks.

Valley of Rocks.

5 After 170 metres of roadwork we pass a signpost that says 'coast path'. Carry along the road, which is starting to ascend; look down towards Lee Bay. Pass over a cattle grid opposite an old toll-house after 440 metres, keeping on the side of the road; another 360 metres takes us past the Christian retreat of Lee Abbey.

6 At 200 metres we leave the road and go through a path on the left; follow the sign in the direction of Six Acre Cross (SW). The

In 1898 a narrow gauge railway was built from Barnstaple to Lynton; it closed in 1935.

path starts to ascend. Keep on the main track through the mixed deciduous wood, after 440 metres turn sharp left and carry on ascending in the direction of Six Acres Cross (NE).

7 After 750 metres we come to a sharp right bend that takes us through Six Acre Wood (SW). Pass through what looks like an old quarry and at 520 metres we pass through a gate and emerge onto open moorland. Keep on the path. After 380 metres pass through the remains on an old gate with the posts there to remind you of the use farmers in the past made of local standing stones. Six-Acre Farm is ahead of us, while Caffyns Heaton Farm can be seen across the wooded combe on our right.

8 Walk past the farm onto a tarmac lane with an honour guard of willows on both sides. After 1100 metres we get to a gate and turn left into Lydiate Lane (NE), passing a motor-home site on our left.

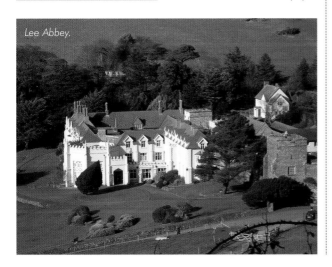

Lee Abbey.

Gate post.

field system that has resisted the prairie-like look of East Anglia.

(10) We pass a collection of old sheds on our right at 750 metres and the road starts to descend. After 330 metres the lane starts to get steeper and the red-tiled roofs of Lynton come into view. We eventually join the road to Lynton at Station Hill.

The poet Shelley spent some time living in Lynton during the early years of his first marriage. Wordsworth, sister Dorothy and Coleridge also visited the town.

Follow signs to the town centre before arriving back at the car park.

(9) After 200 metres we arrive at Dean Cross and take the lane signposted Lynton; it says it is unsuitable for motors. There are expansive views towards Brendon Common: different shades of green, browns, deep valleys folded into the moors and a

Lynton.

Brian Pearce

6 Brendon Hills

A strenuous 7½ mile hike through the glorious countryside
of the eastern edge of Exmoor.

The Brendon Hills lie in the eastern part of Exmoor and provide a gentler alternative to the fiercely bleak moorlands further west. Here there are rolling hills, tree-covered combes and great swathes of woodland, much of it criss-crossed by easily followed paths. The Brendon Hills are also home to the remains of one of Exmoor's flirtations with industrialism – fields are dotted with the ruined nineteenth-century buildings when iron ore was mined in the area; our walk also crosses the steeply inclined, long disused railway line that travelled down to the coast at Watchet.

Level: ♥♥♥♥
Length: 3-7½ miles
Terrain: Even though it starts off relatively undemanding, this walk also takes in combes and hillsides, plus relatively steep descents and ascents through woodland. The reward, however, is a gloriously refreshing and invigorating walk through some of Exmoor's more secretive paths plus a stroll through a part of its industrial history. For a gentler perambulation, there is a family-friendly circuit of approximately three miles.
Park & start: Parking verge on right side of B3190, 200 metres west of Ralegh's Cross Inn.
Start ref: ST034345.
Postcode: TA23 0LN.
Public transport: None
Refreshments: Ralegh's Cross Inn, www.raleghscross.co.uk.

1 After parking (see page 37) walk back along the road in the direction of the Ralegh's Cross Inn, taking great care. Beware: this is a fast road, so keep on the verge. Cross the road opposite the nursery and follow the level track sign-posted Tripp Farm. The track takes a slight curve to the left at 500 metres, passing a barn on the right; 460 metres further note the smooth bulge at the top of the field on the right. This is all that remains of Tripp Barrow.

2 The view ahead (SSE) takes in the Blackdown Hills in the far distance, plus the much closer valleys and woods surrounding Clatworthy Reservoir; a glimpse of its silver-grey surface can usually be had.

Clatworthy Reservoir.

3 Turn right through a gate at 600 metres. Walk westwards keeping the old hedgeline on your left. Another gate leads into Stolford Wood; note the old and blasted tree on the hill opposite.

4 After 160 metres and another gate we follow a track (SW)

Stolford Wood.

Looking towards Stolford Farm.

Hollow way that leads to Brown Lane.

metres barns and what looks like an old railway carriage come into view. Go through the gate ahead into a lane, passing a small pond on the left (WNW). Pass Stolford Farm on the right then turn right into a gate which has 'public bridleway' written on it. Carry on up the track, which eventually becomes a rather attractive hollow way.

6 At 280 metres we pass through another gate. Continue on the hollow way, whose sides are almost like natural sculptures as soil falls exposing roots. We

Ralegh's Cross Inn used to be a meeting place for drovers and pack-horse riders.

through mixed woodland of birch, oak, ash and beech. We arrive at a spring after 350 metres. Cross the spring, go through the gate opposite and follow the path ahead (SW), keeping the fence to our left.

5 Keep to the path with the fence on the left; it can get somewhat marshy here. After 200

eventually get to a gate and Brown Lane. Turn right onto this quiet road, passing over Lower Beverton Bridge after 330 metres; the Beverton is the source of the River Tone.

7 If you want to finish the walk now, turn right after 400 metres and a further field on turn right again, heading east to Tripp Lane and back to the car. Otherwise continue along Brown Lane until the

Huish Champflower Barrow.

Iron ore has been mined on the Brendon Hills for centuries, but the nineteenth century saw a concerted effort to exploit the ore. A railway was built down to Watchet. Part of the journey took in the steep incline to Comberow – it closed at the end of that century.

B3190. Before reaching the road, note the field on the left with Huish Champflower Barrow and its magical circle of trees.

8 At the junction, cross the road, head left towards Beulah Chapel. Turn right, following the road sign-posted North Devon; be careful, as there is no verge. After 300 metres turn right into a field sign-posted Leigh Barton. Descend down the field keeping in line with the fence to the left. After 190 metres turn left into the second gate. We move into woodland, passing a plantation of young trees on our right (NW).

Beulah Chapel.

The Old Mineral Line looking down towards Comberow.

and starts to ascend. After 200 metres the slope inclines to the right, keep going in this direction — with the help of blueway marks we get to a footpath signed 'Leigh Barton ¾ mile' (NW). Start to descend.

 10 Follow the path through woodland; after 300 metres we get

to a track running left to right, cross this and follow the path into dense woodland (NNW). We come to a stile. Climb into an open stretch of field. Make for the stile opposite and into Broadfield Wood we go. In the wood cross a stream then take an ascending path through the woodland (ESE), passing at one stage an old quarry.

9 After 480 metres a gate leads into thicker woodland, keep on the path (NW). Follow the directions to Leigh Barton and after 140 metres we arrive at the Old Mineral Line — note the steep incline. Walk ahead on a path that climbs through woodland, then turns onto a track (N) with a field on the left; blueway marks also help. This track is wide

Leigh Barton Wood.

Brian Pearce

One of the supposed origins of the name Ralegh's Cross is that the body of Simon de Raleigh, lord of nearby Nettlecombe Manor, rested there on its final journey home in 1387.

11 This can be a muddy walk after heavy rain so be prepared. The path soon opens out and on our right is Comberow, down through where the old mineral line used to pass. After 300 metres we pass farm buildings to our right. Keep to the level path.

12 After 100 metres we get to a signpost; follow in the direction of Comberow. The path wheels to the right, and then descends a few metres. Turn right at the bottom of this path and there is a signpost for the B3190. Follow it to the left then as it bears to the right.

13 In 270 metres we get to a track; the white house on the left was apparently the stationmaster's. We soon arrive at a road and cross it taking a track into the woods (S). This is the steepest climb of the walk. Turn sharp right and follow the track up (NNW). After 100 metres it curves to the left (SSE) and levels out. Now turn right (NW) before another turn to the left. After 220 metres turn left again (ESE). This is a great zigzag of a path, which keeps climbing and gets the heart pounding.

14 The path turns sharp right after 200 metres, then sharp left. When we get to two tracks, take the one to the right (W). After 200 metres this curves to the left and soon a field can be seen through the serried ranks of trees. Follow the path through the last few trees and we get to a track that leads us onto the B3190. Turn left and walk to the car.

A slice of woodland magic.

7 Dunkery Beacon

An occasionally demanding 6½-mile perambulation up the highest part of Exmoor with a return through some beautiful combes.

This is a pleasing, invigorating and occasionally challenging hike up the heather-covered slope of Dunkery Beacon and across the roof of Exmoor, with magnificent views of the Bristol Channel and Wales and the Vale of Porlock to the north, while the Quantock Hills and the north Somerset coast stand sentinel to the northwest.

Exmoor, naturally, takes up the views to the south, though on exceptionally clear days we can see Dartmoor and the faint shadows of Dorset hills. The route also takes us past the Bronze Age barrows of Little and Great Rowbarrow, then up onto Stoke Pero Common before a delightful trail back through the combes that cut their way down on the north-western slopes of Dunkery Beacon.

Level: 🌲 🌲
Length: 6½ miles
Terrain: At 519 metres Dunkery Beacon is the highest part of Exmoor so this is very much a walk on the roof of the moor, with far reaching views in all directions — for that reason it's definitely wise to choose a decent day for your perambulation. Even though we are closer to heaven than to earth, the ascent is relatively gentle; however, there are steeper up-and-downs through the combes on the northern side of the walk.
Park & start: There are several parking spaces on the verge of the road that goes up from Dunkery Gate, skirting the eastern flank of the Beacon.
Start ref: SS892416.
Public transport: None.
Refreshments: The Rest and be Thankful at nearby Wheddon Cross (www.restandbethankful.co.uk); pubs and tearooms at Exford.

43

1. Park then briefly walk up the road, following the sign pointing to Dunkery Beacon. After 220 metres we turn left onto a path signed towards the Beacon (WSW).

Brian Pearce

The slopes of Dunkery.

Dunkery Beacon.

2. This is a very clearly marked path, which enables us to admire the magnificent views of surrounding countryside.

3. The path starts a gentle ascent after 640 metres; at 570 metres take the branch to the right with the cairn atop Dunkery ahead. We reach the summit after 160 metres.

4. We now continue along the ridge (W), following the slightly stony path towards the ancient stone barrow of Little Rowbarrow, which we reach after

Cloutsham was originally built as a hunting lodge for the Acland family.

1300 metres. Continue along the path (W) and 360 metres later we get to Great Rowbarrow.

 The path now starts to curve to the right (NW) and after 320 metres it starts a gentle descent through heather and moorland grass — there are views westwards over Stoke Pero and Exford Commons.

 After 360 metres we arrive at the road that

travels down to Horner Woods. Turn right and walk on the verge (NE) — Dunkery Beacon dominates the view to our right, an impressive and dramatic landscape rising to the sky. This is a quiet road though it would be best to keep dogs on the lead. The walk descends. Stoke Pero is ahead on the left and there is a lovely church there is you want to take a detour.

Otherwise, after 1000 metres we turn right, descending

When Queen Victoria's Diamond Jubilee was celebrated in 1897, 44 beacons could be seen from Dunkery.

and following a path (ESE). A few metres on take the right path down into Bagley Combe. After 270 metres we pass over a stream, next to which a large Scots pine stands. The path starts to climb to the left.

Follow the rocky path and after 380 metres take the rutted track to the left (E). After a gentle ascent the path drops and loops into Sweetworthy Combe. We cross a stream, passing a gathering

Stoke Pero Common.

of beeches, oaks and hawthorns and start to climb out of the combe.

(9) Keep to the main path, noting the row of mature beeches to the left. After 270 metres we pass old enclosures with trees growing out of the walls on the left. The walk is easy going at the moment.

Brian Pearce

Horner Water.

In Lorna Doone *Jan Ridd watched the Doones 'firing' Dunkery Beacon to celebrate a new 'captain'.*

(10) After 410 metres the path descends with the steep-sided Aller Combe on the left. We cross a spring and follow the path ahead, which passes through a delightful woodland of birch, oak and holly. We are now travelling along Dickie's Path and after 240 metres there is a view down towards Cloutsham.

(11) After 570 metres the path passes through Hollow Combe; this is a beautiful steep-sided combe with hordes of venerable trees trooping down the hillside of the East Water Valley. Ahead of us we can also see Horner Woods in the distance, which is renowned as a great place to spot red deer.

(12) The path ascends, we cross a spring and come out of the wood. After 410 metres we take the path right (NE) and not long afterwards hit the road. Turn right here and walk along it with Luccombe Hill on our left and Dunkery Beacon on the right. After 1500 metres we return to the car.

The Beacon was left to the National Trust along with the Holnicote Estate, which was owned by the Acland family.

8 Lorna Doone Country

A bracing 7¾-mile circuit that starts off in Lorna Doone country

This is a walk of contrasts that offers stirring views of Forland Point, the aptly named Desolate Point and over the Bristol Channel towards South Wales, as well as the more luxuriant sights of the hidden Doone Valley with its landscape of moorland, heather, gorse and woodland. It can be bracing in parts, while some road work is involved, but the compensation includes a delightful riverside walk, Sisters' Fountain and the remarkable gate posts at the entrance to Glenthorne House. And, of course, the whole area lies at the heart of the classic story *Lorna Doone*.

Level: 🐾 🐾
Length: 7¾ miles
Terrain: An exhilarating and often challenging mixture of steep hill walking and steady progress along the South West Coat path takes us through Lorna Doone country and along part of the magnificent North Devon coastline.
Park & start: car park at the back of the Lorna Doone Farm gift shop.
Start ref: SS793478.
Postcode: EX35 6NU.
Public transport: None at the start of the walk, though the Minehead-Lynmouth 39/300 stops at County Gate.
Refreshments: Lorna Doone Farm teashop at Malmsmead.

Old Burrow Hill

sbury
mon

The Combe

East Lyn River

Southern Wood

lon

Lorna Doone Farm

47

1 After parking at Malmsmead behind the 'Lorna Doone Farm' gift shop cross the old stone bridge over Badgeworthy Water. Continue along the road, passing Oare Village Hall; turn left after 400 metres, following the signpost in the direction of County Gate. A short stroll between a huddle of barns

Southern Wood near Malmsmead.

The ford and bridge at Malmsmead.

takes us to two gates; take the right one, which is blueway marked.

2 We arrive at a small bridge over Oare Water. Cross and turn right, a few metres on turn left

The sisters after whom the Sisters' Fountain spring and its stone cross were named were four nieces of the Reverend WS Halliday.

Sign which is close to Sisters' Fountain.

and walk ahead between a fence (left) and an old bank (right). After 270 metres we get to a signpost and climb in the direction of County Gate. The path starts to ascend and follows the edge of the bracken- and gorse-covered hill (N). It's a steep climb that offers views of Malmsmead, Southern Wood and the valley that leads westwards to Brendon.

3 After 440 metres we meet a fence and follow the path along to its right. County Gate comes into view – this stretch of the walk can be rich with the song of spring-time larks.

4 We reach County Gate and 140 metres later cross the A39. Turn left and walk along the

The Reverend WS Halliday built Glenthorne House in the early part of the nineteenth century. He was a notorious practical joker who liked to baffle local antiquarians by burying Roman coins in places on Exmoor where they would be found.

verge for a few metres then right onto to a path, signposted Sisters' Fountain and Coast Path. A few metres on pass through a gate signed Coast Path (N). Here we start to descend a stony track, which could be slippery in icy conditions.

5 At the bottom of the track we arrive at a path and turn right; it is signed Coast Path, Glenthorne Beach and Seven Horns. A few metres on turn left and descend down steps into the contemplative wooded combe called Sisters' Fountain, which is dominated by a large stone cross over the spring. Now climb up the path through a casual gathering of hawthorn, beech, birch and ash (N). After 400 metres we arrive at a drive; turn right through a

Brian Pearce

Above left: *Stone cross at Sisters' Fountain.* Above right: *Glenthorne.*
Below: *Gateposts at entrance to Glenthorne House drive.*

set of gateposts that are decorated with magnificent boars' heads; this is the drive to Glenthorne House.

(6) Keep on the drive, following an old lodge on the left. After 350 metres we come to a signpost in the direction of the Coast Path and Wingate. Turn left onto a well-trodden path, which is a gentle climb before levelling out. Keep on this path, which after 940 metres

Nobody can say for sure if the Doones were actually based on a true local family of marauders, but one author has attempted to link them to a twelfth-century Thane of Argyll.

Views toward Foreland Point.

starts a gentle descent and we soon pass a signpost to Countisbury. Keep on the path.

(7) Cross the steep-sided Wingate Combe where the path curves to the left, crosses a brook and then goes right (N). After 1100 metres, we cross a small wooden bridge over Dogsworthy Combe's spring; the path is curvaceous but remains easy going. The path climbs at 220 metres, is signed Coast Path, and passes through patches of gorse before opening out.

(8) Take the path that forks left. It is signed Countisbury and County Gate and we are on open moorland. The path begins to ascend after 320 metres; in another 280 metres we take the footpath right and

Desolate Farm made headlines in the local press in 2000 when it was sold for twice its asking price, even though it had no mains electricity.

then turn left onto a path that cuts through a patch of heather. A few metres on we get to a rough track and

turn right following the direction of the sign 'foot path'; the farmhouse Desolate is down on our left.

(9) Within 120 metres we go through a gate, still following the track to the left. The landscape is open moorland with magnificent views over the sea. After 440 metres we come to a yellow waymarked gate

County Gate used to be where a gateway marked the boundary between Somerset and Devon. The eighteenth-century cottage was used for many years as an Exmoor National Park visitors' centre.

on the left of the track; go through it into a field and head up to the top keeping the wall on the left.

(10) When we get to the A39 we head left in the direction of County Gate; there is a path on the verge on the other side. At 280 metres we turn right down the road to Leeford and Brendon. This involves roadwork but is a pleasant and gentle

County Gate.

Brian Pearce

Looking down towards Leeford.

pasture, patches of heather, gorse, hedges and woodland.

12 This is an easy to follow path that travels eastwards along the side of the hill. After 1750 metres, following a descent through gorse, we come to steps and follow the path as it curves to the left making for a small combe. Ashton Farm sits on the hill above. The path then passes over a small bridge, turns left and we follow it down as it ascends and turns to the right in a few metres.

13 After 240 metres the path curves to the right – we follow it through a gate and a few metres on we follow a signpost directing us down to the right towards Malmsmead and Oare. This soon

descent; because it is often narrow keep all dogs on lead especially in the tourist season.

11 After 750 metres we turn left in the direction of

Malmsmead, just before Hall Farm. Follow the path (N), making for a large tree. A few metres on turn sharp right, climbing up a well-trodden path. The view from here is of a landscape of hardy hill

Brian Pearce

Malmsmead nestling in the valley.

Lorna Doone Farm.

becomes an easy to follow riverside walk that after 920 metres gets us back to the small bridge over Oare Water that we crossed earlier. We retrace our steps back to the 'Lorna Doone Farm' shop and its welcoming tearooms.

9 Winsford

A gentle and undemanding 3½-mile stroll that starts in one of Exmoor's prettiest villages.

Winsford is often called the prettiest village on Exmoor with its thatched cottages and old church standing on the Steep.

This walk offers commanding views of the surrounding steep-sided valley through which the Exe River flows far below. It's a high walk so it's not recommended on a windy day if the kids are coming. Watch out for deer on the slopes of Bye Common, and in autumn rutting stags can be heard calling out (bolving in the Exmoor dialect) to any neighbouring hind. If you want to extend it an option would be crossing Bye Common and descending down to Nethercote before climbing to Staddon Farm and coming down Kemps

Level: 🐾
Length: 3½ miles
Terrain: This is the shortest walk in the book and is intended to be one for all the family to share. There's a fairly gentle ascent while the riverside return to Winsford is delightful.
Park & start: Park in Winsford.
Start ref: SS907351.
Postcode: TA24 7JE.
Public transport: The 398 runs between Minehead and Tiverton and makes a couple of stops a day in Winsford.
Refreshments: Royal Oak, Winsford (www.royaloak-somerset.co.uk); Bridge Cottage Tearoom (www.bridgecottageexmoor.co.uk).

Lane to Larcombe Foot and continuing onto Winsford.

1. Park in the middle of Winsford and walk straight up Ash Lane after going over the ford (WNW) and passing the church on the right. The view is across to Burrow Wood, the Punchbowl and Winsford Hill.

2. After 570 metres of a steady ascent on the road, we get to a gate on the right. Follow the path sign-posted Exford and Larcombe Millennium Wood.

3. The path forks left after 120 metres and we keep climbing in the direction of Exford. Enjoy the view of the valley below to the right with the silvery thread of the Exe wending its way towards Winsford. The surrounding landscape is a classic Exmoor one of old

The Royal Oak Inn in Winsford.

Brian Pearce

hedge banks, hill pasture and mixed woodland.

4. We get to a wooden gate and pass through it, climbing higher and higher.

5. After 620 metres we come to a gate, turn left and a few metres above there is a signpost — follow the direction in which it points, keeping to the northern edge of the field (NWW). Bye Hill is on our left.

6. Follow the path and keep climbing and after 280 metres we get to a gate. Here there are glorious views over several deep

valleys some of which are home to isolated farms; Dunkery Beacon glowers in the distance.

7 Follow the direction sign to the immediate right, go through another gate and then left on the path. Note the old stone wall on the left of the path.

Larcombe Millennium Wood.

The valley of the River Exe.

Winsford has six bridges, which cross both the Exe and the Winn Brook, from which it takes its name.

8 Keep on the path and after 400 metres down below us is Larcombe Millennium Wood as well as the place where Larcombe Brook meets its destiny with the Exe; keep an eye out for deer.

9 Passing through another gate, we follow a path with a fence

Bye Common.

to the left and after 400 metres we get to a five-bar gate that leads onto Bye Common. At this point we turn right and follow a track, which leads down the bracken-covered, steep-sided hill, all the way to the Exe at the bottom of the valley. Here turn right, walk a few metres in the direction of the road and turn right just before; follow the signs to Winsford.

10 This is an enchanting and pleasing riverside walk all the way back to Ash Lane and Winsford. After 300 metres the path gently ascends, while the river sings its

The Royal Oak is one of the most photographed country inns in England.

beautiful song to the right. A few metres on it levels out. Parts of it can be very muddy after rain. The path starts descending again and then gets right close to the river.

11 After 400 metres we get to a gate — on the other side of the river stands Northern Mill cottage. This dwelling, along with others in the valley, did not receive mains electricity until 2000.

12 After 170 metres we pass a small stone embankment on the river and the path starts to climb, then levels out as it passes through woodland. Further on the path takes us through a collection of conifers, Scots pine and deciduous trees. Some of them are old and gnarled, once

coppiced but now grown out. Another 170 metres sees the path start to climb and we soon come to the gate through which we pass onto Ash Lane. Follow the road down back into Winsford.

Brian Pearce

Winsford Church.

10 Dulverton

Some steep ascents plus gentle riverside walking makes
this 8½-mile truly rewarding.

Dulverton is a charming small town
that is often seen as the southern
'gateway to Exmoor'. This bracing
walk starts off with the sound of the
Barle River singing away as we climb
above it, before taking off up and
down Exmoor dale.

Even after less than a mile out of town,
you will feel as if you are in splendid
rural isolation. There are views over the
town, towards Pixton House as well as
the Barle Valley as it rushes to meet
the Exe Valley. Further on, after a
selection of combes, the walk passes
beneath a comforting canopy of
woodland, whilst taking
company with, first of all,
Dane's Brook, and
then the sparkling,
bubbling, broad-
shouldered
Barle as it
strolls

down back to Dulverton.

Level: 🌳🌳
Length: 8½ miles
Terrain: The walk starts off with a lung-busting ascent of the 'chimney'; otherwise it's a mix of gradual ascents and descents, well-marked paths (some more stony than others) and a touch of roadwork.
Park & start: There are two car parks in Dulverton, including one by Exmoor House down by the river.
Start ref: SS912278.
Postcode: TA22 9HJ.
Public transport: The 398 runs between Minehead and Tiverton and the 25 connects with Taunton.
Refreshments: There is a good selection of several pubs, tearooms and restaurants in Dulverton.

Map labels: River Barle, Whiterocks Down, East Anstey Common, Bye Hill, Dulverton, 5, 6, 7, 8, 10, 11, 12, 4, 3, 2, 1

1 We start from the old bridge over the Barle opposite the Bridge Inn. Cross and turn first right following directions to Hawkridge. We walk up the road between Rose Cottage and Berry House, bear right

Dulverton Bridge.

It is believed that Mounsey and Brewer's Castle were built in the Iron Age.

at High Corner onto a rougher track and turn left at Horner Cottage. This is a steep climb up an often muddy and stony track, which is locally known as the 'chimney'.

2 After 270 metres, we get to the top and turn left. We go through the gate and walk up the field with the hedge line to the right (W). We arrive at a gate and cross a track that leads to Old Berry Farm on the right. Pass through the gate opposite and follow the path that goes through the middle of the field (W).

Mature oak trees above Lower Chilcott Wood.

3 After 280 metres we go through a gate into another field, following the path with the old tree line on the left (WNW). We arrive at a fence and walk a few metres down to the right where there is a stile. Cross the stile and we are on a road; turn right and walk 150 metres. Go through the gate on the left and walk through the middle of the field down into a combe in the direction of a pair of mature oak trees.

4 After 400 metres we get to a gate, passing a spring and a pond on the right. The path runs ahead, parallel with woodland on the left. Follow the path as it curves to the right, following a small brook on our left. We come to a footbridge. Cross the brook and follow the path as it ascends away to the right. After 280 metres we pass through a gate, and immediately turn right through a gate

Dulverton was originally known as Dieglaford, which meant the 'hidden ford'.

into another field. We follow the path (WSW) to the corner of the field where we pass through a gate onto Chilcott Lane. Turn right.

5 The road ascends past a group of buildings, including Pine Lodge Stables; after 270 metres we pass a track to Cawkett Farm on the left but next left we go through a gate into a field. Walk down the field with the hedgeline to the left (SW), making for a combe ahead. The route descends and after 440 metres we cross a stream and join a path that goes to the right. A few metres on,

where a conduit has been laid in the stream and turfed over, follow the path as it climbs through a gathering of young beeches.

6 We make for a small gate at the top of the field and follow the path across the field to the gate directly opposite. We now arrive on a small road. Turn right and walk for 640 metres, passing the newly-built Chilton House.

7 We get to a junction. Turn left and a few metres on at Five Cross Ways turn right to walk along the road in the direction of Hawkridge.

8 This is easy road walking, on a quiet beech hedge lined carriageway. After 1200 metres turn

Brian Pearce

Dane's Brook.

9 The path continues to descend, passing through a gate into mixed woodland of ash and beech; after 350 metres we get to a wooden bridge over the Dane's Brook. Cross the bridge and follow the path ahead (N); a few metres on follow the directions towards Dulverton. The Dane's Brook is on the right.

During the flood of August 1952, when Lynmouth was devastated, the Barle swept through Dulverton causing flooding while the Golden Guernsey Milk Bar, near the bridge, collapsed as a result.

right into a field following the direction towards Dulverton. The track veers to the right then passes through a line of trees. Follow the directions towards Dane's Brook (N)

through bunches of gorse. After passing through a long line of mature beeches, the path descends — Dane's Brook Valley and Venford Wood can be seen ahead.

Castle Bridge.

10 After 1800 metres walking on this occasionally stony track, we pass Brewer's Castle on the left, an old Bronze Age fort. We then arrive at Castle Bridge. Here we will follow the Barle all the way back to Dulverton.

11 This is an easily identified track that runs alongside the Barle, sometimes on the same level, other times above. It has several easy descents, but it is a glorious and enchanting walk. Sometimes it is out in the open, at other times we pass through a mix of deciduous and evergreen woodland; the enigmatically named New Invention is passed just before we come to Marsh Bridge Cottage after 3360 metres.

Brian Pearce

The River Barle.

Brian Pearce

Burridge Woods.

(12) Here we turn right at the road and walk 270 metres towards Kennel Farm. Turn left in the direction of Dulverton and we now enjoy another stroll alongside the Barle through Burridge Wood until after 2000 metres we arrive back at Dulverton.